LIVING WITH D🐾GS
THERAPY DOGS

HEATHER PIDCOCK-REED

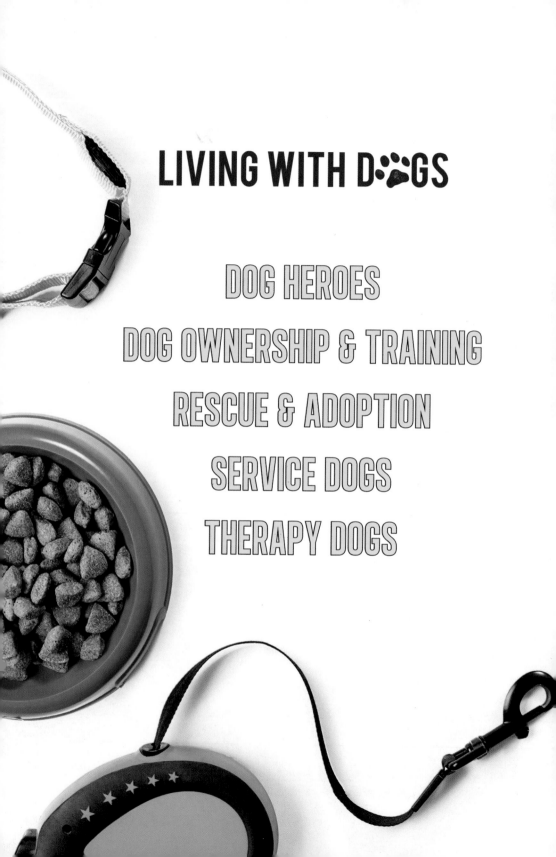

LIVING WITH D🐾GS

DOG HEROES

DOG OWNERSHIP & TRAINING

RESCUE & ADOPTION

SERVICE DOGS

THERAPY DOGS

LIVING WITH D🐾GS

THERAPY DOGS

Heather Pidcock-Reed

MASON CREST

PHILADELPHIA | MIAMI

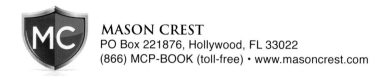

MASON CREST
PO Box 221876, Hollywood, FL 33022
(866) MCP-BOOK (toll-free) • www.masoncrest.com

Printed in the United States of America

First printing
9 8 7 6 5 4 3 2 1

Series ISBN: 978-1-4222-4510-1
Hardcover ISBN: 978-1-4222-4515-6
ebook ISBN: 978-1-4222-7301-2

Cataloging-in-Publication Data on file with the Library of Congress

Developed and Produced by National Highlights, Inc.
Editor: Jacqueline Havelka—Inform Scientific
Cover and Interior Design: Torque Advertising + Design
Layout: Priceless Digital Media

Publisher's Note: Websites listed in this book were active at the time of publication. The publisher is not responsible for websites that have changed their address or discontinued operation since the date of publication. The publisher reviews and updates the websites each time the book is reprinted.

QR CODES AND LINKS TO THIRD-PARTY CONTENT

You may gain access to certain third-party content ("Third-Party Sites") by scanning and using the QR Codes that appear in this publication (the "QR Codes"). We do not operate or control in any respect any information, products, or services on such Third-Party Sites linked to by us via the QR Codes included in this publication, and we assume no responsibility for any materials you may access using the QR Codes. Your use of the QR Codes may be subject to terms, limitations, or restrictions set forth in the applicable terms of use or otherwise established by the owners of the Third-Party Sites. Our linking to such Third-Party Sites via the QR Codes does not imply an endorsement or sponsorship of such Third-Party Sites or the information, products, or services offered on or through the Third-Party Sites, nor does it imply an endorsement or sponsorship of this publication by the owners of such Third-Party Sites.

CONTENTS

KEY ICONS TO LOOK FOR:

Words to Understand: These words with their easy-to-understand definitions will increase the reader's understanding of the text while building vocabulary skills.

Sidebars: This boxed material within the main text allows readers to build knowledge, gain insights, explore possibilities, and broaden their perspectives by weaving together additional information to provide realistic and holistic perspectives.

Educational Videos: Readers can view videos by scanning our QR codes, providing them with additional educational content to supplement the text. Examples include news coverage, moments in history, speeches, iconic sports moments, and much more!

Text-Dependent Questions: These questions send the reader back to the text for more careful attention to the evidence presented there.

Research Projects: Readers are pointed toward areas of further inquiry connected to each chapter. Suggestions are provided for projects that encourage deeper research and analysis.

Series Glossary of Key Terms: This back-of-the-book glossary contains terminology used throughout this series. Words found here increase the reader's ability to read and comprehend higher-level books and articles in this field.

WORDS TO UNDERSTAND

cardiovascular: relating to the heart and blood vessels
cognitive: relating to or involving conscious intellectual activity
psychological: relating to or affecting the mental or emotional state of a person

CHAPTER 1

What Is a Therapy Dog?

How Therapy Dogs Came to Be

The special relationship between people and dogs began thousands of years ago. While no one can know for certain, scientists believe this bond developed when the ancestors of modern dogs began to hang around the homes of ancient peoples in order to scavenge food scraps. At some point, the people began to see that the dogs were useful for protecting their homes and livestock.

Over time, the animals became more domesticated. Ancient dogs were bred to herd livestock, protect property, and assist with hunting. They became an integral part of the daily life of ancient peoples. It wasn't long before they also became valued as companions. Ancient civilizations all around the world began to see the benefit of having dogs as companions and family members.

In addition to enjoying the companionship of dogs, the ancients also began to see that having animals around had some **psychological** and emotional benefits. The first instances of the ancients using animals to improve the mental and emotional well-being of people is recorded in ancient Greece, where the Greeks began to use horses to improve the emotional outlook of people who were gravely ill. For many years, horses were the primary deliverer of these kinds of benefits (and they are still utilized in this capacity today).

It wasn't until the 1800s that nurse Florence Nightingale began to notice that small pets reduced anxiety and stress in both young and old patients. These observations led to research on what came to be known as the human-animal bond.

Sigmund Freud had a chow named Jofi that looked very much like this one. Jofi kept Freud's patients at ease.

Dr. Levinson's worked paved the way for therapy dogs like this one to be utilized in a number of different environments.

According to the American Veterinary Medical Association (AVMA), "the human-animal bond is a mutually beneficial and dynamic relationship between people and animals that is influenced by behaviors considered essential to the health and well-being of both. The bond includes, but is not limited to the emotional, psychological, and physical interactions of people, animals, and the environment." The early stages of this research led the Austrian neurologist and founder of modern psychoanalysis, Sigmund Freud, to begin using his dog Jofi in his sessions.

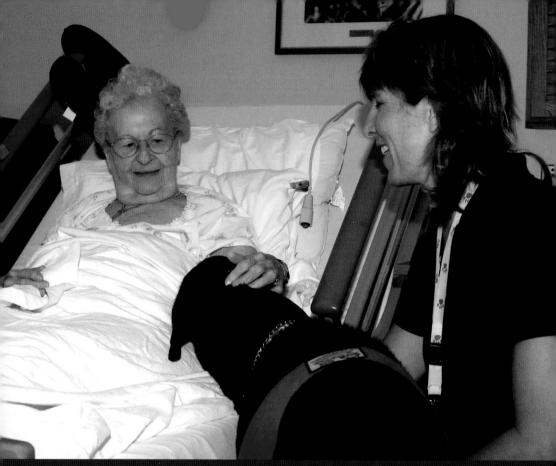

This therapy dog is visiting a hospice patient.
Therapy dogs can bring a great deal of comfort to
those in hospitals, nursing homes, and hospices.

In the 1960s, child psychologist Dr. Boris Levinson began to conduct formal research on using animals in therapy. Dr. Levinson discovered that his own dog had a positive impact on his young patients who had mental impairments. These patients seemed to feel more comfortable with the dog around and also to prefer socializing with the dog than with other people. Unfortunately, Dr. Levinson's work wasn't taken seriously until after the publication of Freud's journals and letters detailing his work with Jofi several decades earlier. Dr. Levinson then became known as the "Father of Animal-Assisted Therapy."

Therapy Dogs

Initially, the idea of therapy dogs was met with laughter and derision from those in the field of psychology. However, Sigmund Freud (one of the founders of modern psychology) often utilized his beloved Chow-Chow Jofi in his therapy sessions. While Jofi was initially present during these sessions because Freud found that he himself was calmer with the dog nearby, Freud observed that many of his patients also seemed more at ease when Jofi was present. According to an article in *Psychology Today*, Freud noted that these differences were most pronounced in children or adolescents, and that patients in general were more willing to talk openly about painful issues when a dog was in the room.

Freud began experimenting by placing Jofi in various places around the room. This allowed him to observe that placing Jofi in a location near the patient tended to result in the patient being able to discuss their emotions more easily. He also found that placing Jofi near himself and away from the patient resulted in no benefit for the patient. A paper published on the history of therapy dogs states that Freud used Jofi to facilitate doctor-patient communication. Conversations with Jofi present often served as a stepping-stone to patients feeling comfortable enough to speak with Freud himself.

These discoveries, made in the 1930s, weren't researched until almost two decades after Freud's death in 1939. This is because most of Freud's experimentation with Jofi was detailed in private letters and journals that weren't uncovered until after he died. While it took some time for this practice to catch on, the work that Freud did with Jofi was essential in establishing the function of a therapy dog and would help make this growing movement more respectable within the field of mental health care.

Once Dr. Levinson's work was validated, the utilization of animals in therapeutic settings became more popular. By 1989, the Delta Society, a group dedicated to animal education, had created a certification program for therapy animals. This was to ensure that dogs (along with other animals) with the title of "therapy dog" would be held to some kind of standard. There are now a number of different certification programs; however, they all adhere to the basics that were put in place by the Delta Society.

What Are Therapy Dogs and What Do They Do?

The Alliance of Therapy Dogs states that a therapy dog is one that has been trained "to provide psychological or physiological therapy to individuals other than their handlers." These canines must have stable temperaments, easy-going personalities, and the ability to

A therapy animal must be able to deal with being handled by people it doesn't know well.

work in multiple environments. Some may work in a therapist's office, providing support to patients in the same way that Freud's dog Jofi did. Others work in schools, hospitals, nursing homes, rehabilitation centers, group homes, and daycares. They are even utilized to provide emotional support to victims of natural disasters.

In recent years, therapy dogs have also been brought into communities to assist students and family members who have been impacted by tragedies like school shootings. According to the Alliance of Therapy Dogs, these animals were used after the Sandy Hook Elementary School shooting in Newtown, Connecticut. In that horrific event, twenty-six people—twenty students and six adults—were shot and killed. Among the first responders on the scene were therapy dogs to help grieving and overwhelmed children and parents.

Therapy dogs are typically owned by a person who enjoys volunteering in places and situations like the above. Their primary function is to provide comfort and happiness to the people they work with. An animal involved in therapeutic work should be calm, friendly, and able to work with an array of people. Not every dog is cut out to be a therapy dog, and that is ok.

Most places that allow people to bring in therapy dogs like to see that the animal has some type of certification. This ensures that the dog has been properly trained and tested in delivering this kind of support to people. These certifications are typically not that difficult to obtain and require you to demonstrate that an animal has basic obedience skills and a friendly temperament and is comfortable being handled by strangers.

As we will explore in a later chapter, therapy dogs are not the same as service dogs. However, some service dogs may be trained as therapy dogs as well. The important thing to remember is that therapy dogs are trained to work with multiple people who are not their owners.

What Kinds of Benefits Do Therapy Dogs Provide?

A number of different studies have been conducted in recent years that show that the mere act of petting a dog can significantly reduce the amount of stress that a person feels. The calming effect of being around a pet and interacting with it releases a hormone known as oxytocin, also known as the "love hormone." The purpose of this hormone is to increase and strengthen bonds between people. This, in combination with the powerful ability of dogs to reduce the

The simple act of petting a dog has been scientifically proven to reduce stress. The work that therapy dogs do provides us with comfort and happiness.

production of stress hormones, leads to better physical and mental health in people.

These discoveries explain why therapy dogs are so effective. Therapy animals provide people who may not be able to have a pet with the same benefits of pet ownership. Recent studies performed on animal-assisted therapy show that in addition to providing comfort and emotional support, therapy dogs also provide **cardiovascular,** psychological, and **cognitive** benefits.

The cardiovascular benefits obtained from therapy animals are the result of the reduction of stress levels. Lower levels of stress lead to fewer instances of heart problems. In fact, there are a number of studies that have shown that people who have contact with dogs after having a heart attack or stroke are less likely to have another event. It is therefore beneficial for patients suffering from heart disease or other related medical issues to have contact with therapy dogs as part of their rehabilitation.

Scan here to view a short video about how therapy dogs can help people in a rehabilitation setting.

The psychological benefits of animal-assisted therapy are numerous. Studies have found that this therapy really helps to ease anxiety and elevate mood, improve social and communication skills, facilitate independent living, and heighten empathy. In general, interactions with animals promote positive emotions, which in turn boost confidence and reduce loneliness, sadness, anger, and insecurity. Just petting a dog can help people feel less lonely and more positive about life in general. These positive feelings can assist in developing an environment of healing for people going through difficult times. As you can imagine, this makes animal-assisted therapy a useful treatment method for people who suffer from mental illnesses such as depression and anxiety.

Another interesting advantage of therapy dogs is that they can provide cognitive benefits to people. Studies performed on dementia patients who interacted with therapy dogs found that there was a decrease in the agitation and aggression found in many with dementia, along with an increase in verbal responses and engagement. Other studies have found that therapy dogs can be beneficial to cognitive development in children. For instance, children who are able to interact with a therapy dog have shown improved reading skills, memory, and problem-solving skills. The cognitive benefits provided by therapy dogs are evident in people of all ages and cognitive abilities.

Of course, these are only a few of the many benefits that therapy dogs provide. The list will most likely grow as researchers continue to study the therapeutic impact of these animals on human beings. However, this research only serves to give us scientific evidence of what most dog lovers have been saying for thousands of years—that our canine companions offer us so much more than we initially intended them to. Not only are they able to help us in farming, hunting, guarding, and other endeavors, but they are also able to assist us in living happier and healthier lives.

TEXT-DEPENDENT QUESTIONS

1. Where might you find a therapy dog at work?
2. What does a therapy dog do?
3. What are the benefits of working with therapy dogs?

RESEARCH PROJECT

Go to the library or use the internet to research the benefits that therapy dogs can have on mental health. Write a three-page informative essay explaining the ways that these animals can help in treating mental illnesses. Remember to cite your sources.

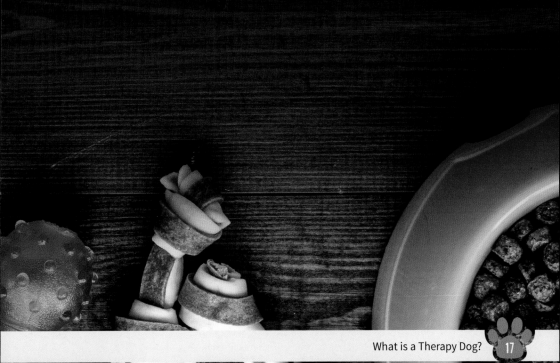

WORDS TO UNDERSTAND

executive functioning: the cognitive ability to plan, focus, remember, and juggle several tasks at a time

Fair Housing Act: legislation in the United States that prohibits discrimination against someone renting or buying a house

neurological: relating to the nerves and nervous system

social-emotional skills: the ability to understand, experience, manage, and express emotions

CHAPTER 2

Types of Therapy Dogs

What Kinds of Dogs Can Be Therapy Dogs?

Any dog can be a therapy dog if it has the right temperament. There are no breed or size restrictions. A therapy dog can be large or small, purebred or mixed breed. It can be a dog that you got as a puppy or that you adopted as an adult from a shelter or rescue. What matters most is that it is friendly, well mannered, well trained, calm, and able to interact nicely with a variety of strangers from different walks of life. Not shedding excessively is also a trait that is good for these animals to have (although it is not necessary).

While therapy dogs can be any size, smaller breeds are particularly well suited for the job, especially when it comes to doing work in hospitals or nursing homes. This is due to their small size, which allows them to be easily lifted up and placed into beds or onto the laps of the people they are visiting. Another reason smaller breeds or mixes tend to do well as therapy dogs is because many of the smaller-sized breeds were initially bred to be solely companion animals; therefore, it is in their nature to enjoy sitting on laps, cuddling and being petted by people. All of these traits are essential when it comes to doing therapy work.

However, therapy animals don't have to be small in stature. Larger breeds that are known for their patience and calm demeanor can also perform therapy work well. These breeds include Labrador retrievers, German shepherds, golden retrievers, and collies. As long as the pup has the right temperament and enjoys being handled by different people, it will be a successful therapy dog.

Are There Different Kinds of Therapy Animals?

The job duties of a therapy dog are not as structured as those of a service dog, and there are different types of therapy dogs. Some are more common than others. Many of them are family pets, while some belong to and are owned by the facility where they perform their work. No matter what type of job they perform, all of these canines have the uncanny ability to cheer up and bring comfort to the people they interact with while on the job.

Scan here to watch a video about breeds that make great therapy dogs.

There are no breed or size restrictions when it comes to being a therapy dog. Regardless of their size, therapy dogs quickly become beloved by the people they help.

Therapeutic Visitation Dogs

Therapeutic visitation dogs are the most common type of therapy animal. They are family pets that are brought by their owners into hospitals, nursing homes, rehabilitation facilities, detention facilities, and other places. This is usually done on a volunteer basis. According to Therapy Dogs of Vermont, visitation dogs can really help people who are away from home due to mental or physical illness. These people miss their own pets, so some time spent with a visitation dog can lift spirits and even provide motivation for treatment.

This type of therapy animal is also used in places like schools and colleges to assist students. Recent studies have shown that having a dog in the classroom has several different benefits. For instance, a therapy animal can calm children down, reducing the amount of stress and anxiety that is sometimes felt in a school environment. Its presence also assists in developing a child's **social-emotional skills.** "Loving and lovable, dogs are friendly companions and good listeners who make no judgments," writes teacher Elizabeth Mulvahill. "Children bond easily with these gentle creatures, helping them feel more connected and confident. This leads to a reduction in negative behavior and aggression."

Small dogs are the perfect size when it comes to cuddling on someone's lap. This is one of the reasons many of them make great therapy animals.

Having a therapy dog in class can help children calm down, as well as learn how to deal with their emotions.

In addition to the health and emotional benefits that occur when therapy dogs are present in schools, studies have also shown that there are cognitive benefits. Mulvahill says, "Interacting with therapy dogs improves students' reading skills, stimulates memory and problem-solving skills, and even optimizes **executive-functioning** skills." Mulvahill has observed that a dog's presence in the classroom seems to foster better concentration, attention, motivation, and relaxation in her students. When stress levels are lower, learning is more effective and it shows in student performance.

Animal-Assisted Therapy Dogs

Another type of therapy animal is an animal-assisted therapy dog. These dogs typically work in rehabilitation facilities. They provide

CLASSROOM THERAPY DOG

Mary Ostmoe is an elementary-level special education teacher who wanted to utilize a therapy dog within her classroom environment. She hoped that by doing so, her special education students would feel calmer and focus better in class. After doing some fund-raising within her community, she was able to adopt a golden retriever named Olaf and have him trained by a service dog organization to be a therapy dog. Olaf spends the day at school with Ostmoe and goes home with her each night. Olaf has his own kennel in the corner of Ostmoe's classroom that he rests in when he isn't working with the children.

Ostmoe uses Olaf to help her students talk about their feelings. She lets the students face Olaf and pet him rather than look at her. Petting Olaf reduces their stress, and the students also feel like they are talking to Olaf rather than Ostmoe, which helps them manage their emotions better. The principal at Ostmoe's school occasionally sends non-special education students down to Olaf's classroom when they are having a difficult time.

In addition to calming children down, Olaf's presence has helped encourage the children to read more. Ostmoe says that kids love reading to Olaf and that Olaf also loves reading time. Ostmoe reports that Olaf loves his job. She also says that he has been of benefit to the other students, faculty, and staff at her school. Olaf is nonjudgmental, and Ostmoe says that is what many kids need. Children on the autism spectrum often exhibit behaviors that other children are uncomfortable with, but Olaf doesn't care.

Many schools are somewhat resistant to the idea of having full-time therapy dogs available to students. However, Ostmoe and Olaf are working to make the idea more acceptable. The success that they have had in their school could help to pave the way for more teachers to utilize therapy dogs within their classrooms.

Animal-assisted-therapy dogs can help patients build some of the motor skills required for daily life.

help to patients working with occupational and physical therapists. Patients who visit or live in these types of rehabilitation centers are often recovering from issues such as strokes, physical injuries, surgeries, or other ailments that impact their ability to perform daily tasks. The role of a therapy dog in this setting is to provide not only emotional support but also assistance as patients work to regain abilities like fine motor control or limb movement. These animals play an essential part in assisting patients in recovering so that they can return home to their families.

Animal-assisted therapy dogs may also be utilized by speech therapists, psychologists, special education specialists, and other mental and physical health-care providers. Animal-assisted therapy is commonly used for patients with **neurological** and muscle disorders. According to a recent study, occupational therapists who work with children on the autism spectrum love to work with dogs because treatment with dogs results in improved social skills, motivation, interest in treatment, and self-awareness. Another study found that senior citizens in a walking program at an assisted living facility walked farther when with a dog than when they walked alone, indicating the potential value of pets in physical conditioning.

Facility Therapy Dogs

A facility therapy dog is one that is owned by a facility such as a nursing home or rehabilitation center. It typically works with psychologists, rehabilitation therapists, and other similar

Some long-term residential care facilities have their own resident therapy dog living on the premises.

professionals in a place where patients live full time. These animals help the residents feel more motivated to engage in physical activities, as well as to communicate with those around them better. Facility therapy dogs have been found to be incredibly useful in nursing homes that specialize in caring for patients with Alzheimer's disease.

Another area where a facility therapy dog may be utilized is in a drug or mental health rehabilitation center. These types of facilities often have patients staying there for a period of weeks to months. The function of the therapy dog in these settings is to help patients feel comfortable in a therapeutic setting, much in the same way a therapeutic visitation dog does. They can provide comfort to distressed people and help improve their overall mental health so that their treatments are more effective.

Crisis Response Dogs

A crisis response dog works to comfort people who have experienced some kind of traumatic event. According to the American Kennel Club (AKC), a crisis response dog is specially trained to handle crowded, stressful situations to help people remain calm in disasters. You may have seen coverage on the news about these kinds of dogs being brought in to help people who are struggling with stress and other emotions after a tornado, earthquake, hurricane, or other natural disaster. Crisis response dogs are also utilized in the aftermath of other traumatic events such as mass shootings or acts of terrorism.

These dogs are often owned by individuals or families who volunteer their animals and their time to come and assist others in traumatic situations. They are also frequently associated with nonprofit or government organizations, which bring in the volunteers and their dogs when needed. Crisis response dogs can provide a great deal of comfort to those who are suffering in the midst and aftermath of a crisis.

Emotional Support Dogs

An emotional support dog is a privately owned animal that provides emotional and psychological support to an individual. They are different from therapy dogs because they typically only provide companionship and support to their owners. There are no training or certification requirements for an emotional support animal; however,

Crisis response dogs can help bring comfort to individuals who have been impacted by traumatic events.

Emotional support animals can be trained to provide a great deal of comfort and support to their owners.

there are protections for them under the **Fair Housing Act.** They are also afforded some allowances for flying on airplanes provided you have a letter from your doctor stating that your pet is an emotional support animal.

While not an official therapy dog, an emotional support dog can be incredibly beneficial to people who have mental health problems such as depression, panic attacks, bipolar disorder, post-traumatic stress disorder, and more. An emotional support dog's basic function is providing comfort and unconditional love, but also therapy assistance.

Having a therapy dog to focus on during counseling sessions can help patients feel more comfortable discussing troubling issues they are facing.

TEXT-DEPENDENT QUESTIONS

1. What are the different types of therapy dogs?
2. What is an emotional support dog?
3. What type of dog can be a therapy dog?

RESEARCH PROJECT

Choose one of the types of therapy dogs mentioned in this chapter and conduct research on the kind of work these animals do. Design and make a poster showing this type of dog at work. Write one paragraph defining this type of therapy dog and what it does.

WORDS TO UNDERSTAND

Americans with Disabilities Act (ADA): legislation in the United States that prohibits discrimination against people with disabilities

caveat: a warning of certain limitations

legitimate: legally allowed or acceptable

CHAPTER 3

Therapy Dogs vs. Service Dogs

What Is a Service Dog?

Have you ever been out and about and noticed a dog wearing a "Service Dog" vest? If so, you've seen a service dog at work. You may be wondering what exactly a service dog is. In 1990, the **Americans with Disabilities Act** (ADA) established a legal definition in the United States, which was revised and updated in 2010:

> "Service animals are defined as dogs that are individually trained to do work or perform tasks for people with disabilities. Examples of such work or tasks include guiding people who are blind, alerting people who are deaf, pulling a wheelchair, alerting and protecting a person who is having a seizure, reminding a person with a mental illness to take prescribed medications, calming a person with Post Traumatic Stress Disorder (PTSD) during an anxiety attack, or performing other duties. Service animals are working animals, not pets. The work or task a dog has been trained to provide must be directly related to the person's disability."

This definition limits the title of service animal and the legal protections offered to dogs that have been specifically trained to assist a person with some sort of disability. While the definition may be slightly different from country to country, the one provided by the ADA is similar to most. There are many different tasks that a service dog may perform. These include anything from alerting its owner to an impending anxiety attack to turning lights on and off.

Service dogs perform many different tasks, such as guidance for the blind, hearing assistance, mobility help, autism assistance, diabetic alerts, seizure alerts, seizure response, veteran's assistance, psychiatric help, and more. The possibilities are practically endless. Therefore, the most important thing to remember when it comes to defining a service dog is that it performs essential tasks and services for its person.

Scan here to watch a video about the differences between service, therapy, and emotional support dogs.

Guide dogs are probably one of the most well-known types of service dogs. They assist the blind or visually impaired in navigating their daily lives.

When you come across a service animal while out in public, you should not approach it or pet it, as it is working. If you would like to meet the dog, you should approach its owner and ask if you may pay attention to the animal. This isn't because the animal is unfriendly. It is simply so that it does not become distracted from performing its job.

How Are Therapy Dogs Different from Service Dogs?

Many people use the terms *service dog* and *therapy dog* interchangeably. While therapy dogs and service dogs both help people, there are many differences. These differences have to do with their primary function, as well as with the way they are viewed

Unlike service dogs, therapy dogs aren't allowed to go everywhere. They need permission before being admitted into businesses and other facilities.

on a legal level. On occasion, some of the functions provided by these two types of helper animals will overlap, but it is important that you understand that they are different.

The biggest difference is that therapy dogs aren't offered legal protections like service animals are. For instance, it is illegal for businesses to deny entrance to a service animal. However, a therapy dog can be denied entrance to places. This means that a hospital, school, nursing home, or other facility must approve an animal before it is allowed to come in and work with people.

Service dogs are not considered pets under the law, while therapy dogs are. This means that a person can't be denied housing because of their service animal. Since therapy dogs are considered pets, they aren't guaranteed housing in rental situations. According to the AKC, service dogs are allowed on airplanes and other forms of public transportation free of charge, with one **caveat**—each airline has its own rules regarding service dogs. Most require that the dog sit on the traveler's lap or at their feet, and dogs can't block the aisles or emergency exits.

Another difference between therapy dogs and service dogs is the people that they serve. As we discussed in a previous chapter, therapy dogs generally work with multiple people who are in need of comfort and support. These people are rarely the dog's owner. A service dog is assigned to just one person. While the service animal may provide a great deal of comfort and support to the person, it is trained to perform other tasks to help its owner. In addition, service dogs are usually trained to ignore people who aren't their handler.

The best way to remember the differences between these two types of helping animals is to recall that they both serve different purposes. The purpose of a service dog is to help an individual

Because service dogs help individuals with disabilities, a service dog is usually trained to ignore everyone but their handler when they are working.

disabled person with specific tasks related to their disability. The purpose of a therapy dog is to provide comfort and support to many people.

How Are Emotional Support Dogs Different from Service Dogs?

In an earlier chapter, we discussed how emotional support dogs are different from therapy dogs. Emotional support animals are personal pets that provide comfort and support to their owners. The Alliance of Therapy Dogs states that emotional support animals (ESAs) are prescribed by licensed mental health professionals to provide therapeutic benefits to people with psychological issues

Emotional support dogs are protected under the Fair Housing Act. They are also allowed to fly with their handlers for free.

like anxiety, phobias, or PTSD. Patients must be diagnosed with a disabling mental condition and have certain limitations to qualify for an ESA. Emotional support animals are allowed to live anywhere and are also allowed to accompany their handlers on airplanes. However, they are not given the right to visit any public place.

While there are psychiatric service dogs that work with those with mental illnesses, those dogs are trained to do things like remind the person to take their medication or alert a person that an anxiety attack or flashback episode is about to occur, as well as offer emotional support and comfort. Emotional support animals are not trained to perform the tasks that a service dog is. In fact, emotional support dogs don't have to undergo any sort of training in order to help their person.

Why Is It Important to Understand the Differences?

You might be wondering why it is important to know the difference between service dogs, therapy dogs, and emotional support dogs. While all of these animals provide important services and support to people, their functions are different. This means that the rights and protections afforded to them under the law are different. Since there are no overseeing certifying organizations for service animals and since owners aren't required to show proof that their animal is a service dog, it is important that you know the difference yourself.

Unfortunately, recent years have seen an increase in the number of fake service animals, and this has caused several problems within the service dog community. According to an article in *Florida Today,* many people are registering regular pets as service animals. Untrained animals have caused disruption and have even attacked other dogs and bitten people. This all affects people who own real service dogs, because their animals are now scrutinized as to whether their owners truly need them.

MURRAY: A SHELTER DOG THAT BECAME A THERAPY DOG

When licensed marriage and family therapist Colleen Perry adopted Murray from a local shelter, she had no idea that he would play a large role in the therapy sessions she ran with her clients. Perry discovered that Murray loved going on car rides with her. This led to the animal going just about everywhere with her, including her office. It was then that Perry found Murray had a real knack for comforting her patients—many of whom are dealing with serious issues such as eating disorders, relationship issues, chronic pain, and PTSD.

Perry reports that Murray immediately goes over to comfort anyone who is crying or upset. He will nudge at a patient's leg to make them feel better. If the patient asks him to, he will jump on the couch with them to provide comfort, which helps patients get the most out of their time with Perry.

"I look forward to seeing Murray at every appointment because he is very special to me," says one of Perry's patients. "When I come into the room, he comes up on the couch so I can pet him. It's like he is letting me know that I am loved, and I feel special. I always feel safe with Murray, and I don't feel this way with people. He seems to have a way of knowing when I am upset. Whenever he senses this, he comes over to me and puts his head against my leg, or hops up on the couch, which always makes me feel better."

Murray's presence has truly made a difference in Perry's work with the Soldiers Project. Many of the veterans she assists through this project believe Murray helps them focus and feel safe. Patients refer to Murray as "Dr. Murray," a dog always wagging his tail and ready to greet patients with kind eyes.

Colleen Perry and Murray.

Knowing the difference between service, therapy, and emotional support dogs can help people know how to spot legitimate animals doing their jobs.

These fake service dogs cause business owners and others to question the validity of **legitimate** service dogs. According to the USA Service Dogs registry, people who disguise their pets as service dogs are making life more difficult for people with disabilities.

The same issue exists in the therapy dog and emotional support dog communities. When untrained and ill-behaved pets are posed as being therapy or emotional support animals, they make it harder for the actual dogs performing this work to be accepted. Abusing the system in this manner makes life more difficult for people who genuinely need these types of animals.

"As a veteran with a service dog trained for me by This Able Veteran, I am so utterly exhausted with fake service and support animals," said Carissa Rawson. "I travel a lot. And every time I go somewhere, I am under constant scrutiny—like the star of my very own soap opera—as person after person accuses me of faking, of not looking disabled enough, or of attempting to smuggle my pet on a plane… The explosion of fraudulent service and support animals means that I—an owner of a real service dog suffering with a real disability—am the one paying the price."

Knowing the difference between service, therapy, and emotional support animals helps the community to identify when someone is abusing the system. This in turn assists the people who truly need these dogs in their lives to be better accepted within their communities. It also allows you to educate people on the differences so that they can better understand the amazing ways that all of these dogs can help people.

A legitimate therapy dog is able to comfort others in amazing ways.

There are important differences between regular pets, service dogs, therapy dogs, and emotional support dogs. While all of these animals provide support to people, their functions are very different.

TEXT-DEPENDENT QUESTIONS

1. What is the difference between a therapy dog and a service dog?
2. What types of service dogs are there?
3. Are service dogs considered pets?

RESEARCH PROJECT

Look up the differences between a therapy dog and an emotional support dog. Write a five-paragraph compare-and-contrast essay on the two.

objectively: not influenced by your personal feelings or opinions
self-esteem: confidence in yourself, or the feeling that you are valuable; self-worth
sociable: willing to engage with others

CHAPTER 4

Can Your Dog Be a Therapy Dog?

The Rewards of Owning a Therapy Dog

Owning a therapy dog can be a very rewarding experience. Not only do you get to watch your pup bring a great deal of comfort to those in need, but you also get to be exposed to and help a variety of people from different walks of life. Helping people in need causes a person to have positive feelings about themselves and the world around them. Those warm feelings are what drive many people to volunteer. Therefore, it's no surprise that many dog owners choose to donate their time and their canine companions to help others.

Before you go down the path of having your dog trained and certified as a therapy dog, there are many things you need to consider. While owning and handling a therapy dog is incredibly rewarding, there are some challenging aspects to it. You will find that it takes a certain type of dog and a certain type of owner to be able to handle this type of work.

Not every dog and handler have the right type of personality to be a therapy animal team. Both need to be patient, calm, and able to socialize with strangers.

Is Your Dog's Personality Well Suited for Therapy Work?

Most dogs are friendly and enjoy being around people, especially when those people are willing to pay lots of attention to them. And the majority of dogs do a wonderful job of providing comfort and other forms of emotional support to their owners. However, a friendly, loving dog that is good at helping you in your times of need does not necessarily make a good therapy dog. Therapy dogs need to have a certain kind of personality.

The temperament for a therapy animal is one that is naturally **sociable.** The dog should also be somewhat calm and friendly toward strangers. Professional therapy dog trainer Linda Keehn suggests that you try your best to **objectively** assess your pet's personality and temperament. This is so you can determine whether your pup would actually enjoy working as a therapy dog.

Keehn advises asking yourself whether your dog really enjoys interacting with new people in new situations. Is your dog calm? Does it seek attention from people? Most often in a therapy situation, people just want an animal that sits next to them so they can pet it. If your pup prefers to only receive attention from you or other members of your household, it will most likely not be a good fit as a therapy dog.

If your dog enjoys all kinds of interaction with strangers, it may be a good candidate for therapy work.

Dogs that are friendly and affectionate with strangers are the best candidates. The animal will be in contact with people it may have never met before. A dog that is too shy or reserved will not be able to handle the amount of contact from strangers that a therapy animal receives.

Another good quality to look for in a therapy dog is the ability to adapt to a number of novel situations and noises. After all, your pet will frequently be going to new places and encountering new things in its job as a therapeutic animal. According to an article from the AKC, therapy dogs must handle situations like screaming, elevator rides, and being around different kinds of medical equipment—all without becoming scared, startled, or anxious.

Your pup should also be able to tolerate slight physical discomfort without growling, nipping, or biting. Writer and therapy dog trainer Kathy Santo says, "At one of the very first visits I took my team on, a child got so excited to pet one of the dogs that he put the dog's ear in a viselike grip and it took two aides to extract him." According to animal behaviorist Patricia McConnell, PhD, a good therapy dog must behave in ways that most dogs do not. The dog must remain unfazed when hugged too hard by a child, or when an Alzheimer's patient screams when you try to take it away.

Are You Able to Be a Therapy Dog Handler?

After assessing whether your pet is a good candidate for work as a therapy dog, you need to decide whether you are a good fit. A therapy animal doesn't work alone; it works with you. You and your canine companion will be functioning as a team in whatever environment you choose to work in. This means that you will need to be comfortable putting yourself into a variety of situations with people within your community.

Interacting with people you don't know and engaging in conversations with them are essential parts of being a therapy animal handler. Many hospital patients don't get to interact with many nonmedical people, so the handler may be the only

A great therapy dog handler is able to sit and talk with the people their dog is working with.

nonmedical person they've had a conversation with for days. Handlers need to be prepared to also connect with the client. If you're shy or uncomfortable speaking with strangers, being a handler may not be your best choice.

You also need to be comfortable dealing with people who are experiencing a great deal of pain, sickness, or grief. While not everyone you work with will fall into those categories, it is important that you are comfortable navigating conversations with people in need of comfort. Some of the people you encounter while volunteering with your pup may have been through extremely traumatic events. You should be able to treat them with compassion and dignity, as well as with sensitivity regarding the things they have been through.

On December 14, 2012, a mass shooting occurred at Sandy Hook Elementary School in Newtown, Connecticut. Twenty children between the ages of 6 and 7 and six adults were killed in the shooting. This tragedy had a great impact on the small community of Newtown. In the aftermath of the shooting, a number of comfort and therapy dogs were brought to help the families of the victims and other members of the community as they processed their grief.

Ruthie, a golden retriever and the 2016 ASPCA Dog of the Year, was one of those comfort dogs. Sandy Hook was the first comfort dog assignment that Ruthie went on. She was able to get a number of the children affected to open up and talk to counselors. However, she had a significant impact on Freddy Hubbard, a 9-year-old boy who lost his 6-year-old sister, Catherine, in the shooting. Jenny Hubbard, Freddy and Catherine's mother, explained that animals like Ruthie go into these painful situations, take on people's sadness, and give back love.

Ruthie has gone on to work with people in the aftermath of the Boston Marathon bombing in 2013. She has also worked with families that were impacted by devastating tornadoes, wildfires, and flooding. In addition, she provided comfort to those affected by the nightclub shooting in Orlando in 2016. Richard Martin, co-director of the Lutheran Church Charities K-9 Comfort Dog Ministry, described Ruthie as being very intuitive in keying on peoples' anxiety. She senses it, relaxes, lays her head on people, and just snuggles.

In addition to dealing with people, you also need to be able to read your dog's body language and advocate for your pup when it is becoming mentally and physically tired. McConnell explains that a handler's main job is to eliminate as much of the dog's stress as possible. Once the dog is presented to people, the handler backs off but remains alert to the dog's reactions and to possibly inappropriate interactions. If the handler notices signs of stress in the dog, they must step in and address the situation.

Another consideration is what kind of therapy work you feel comfortable doing. For instance, your dog may love working with children, but you may feel uncomfortable with doing so. In this case, volunteering in a place like a nursing home might be the better option for you. The key to successfully volunteering with your therapy dog is to find a place where you both feel comfortable and at ease.

Scan here to learn more about how Ruthie helped people after Sandy Hook and other tragedies.

The wonderful thing about therapy animal work is that you can choose which settings you and your pup feel most comfortable working in.

Volunteering with your dog can benefit your physical and mental health.

What Are the Benefits of Volunteering with Your Therapy Dog?

Volunteers have a tremendous impact on the communities they serve. Many organizations would not be able to function without them. As we discussed earlier, lending a helping hand to those in need makes you feel good about yourself and others. It also makes your community a better place to live. But did you know that along with helping out your community and the people in it, volunteering with your dog can benefit both your physical and mental health?

A number of studies have found that people who volunteer are likely to live longer lives. A report published by the Corporation for National and Community Service found that those who volunteer over 100 hours a year tend to be much healthier on average than those who don't. Volunteering also appears to reduce a person's risk of developing Alzheimer's and dementia. This is because of the social interaction that occurs.

The physical aspects of volunteering can also help to promote weight loss and reduce your risk of developing heart disease. While some jobs don't require much physical activity, just the act of getting out of your house and doing something promotes a healthier and more active lifestyle.

Volunteering also helps your mental health. It has been shown to have a positive impact on those suffering from mental illness. This is because it allows people to feel connected to others. In addition, many people develop deep friendships with their fellow volunteers. Studies also indicate that donating your time to a cause you believe in can help boost **self-esteem.**

Another often overlooked benefit to volunteering is that it helps you develop skills that you can use in other areas of your life. For instance, when you work with your therapy dog, you will develop social skills while you talk to the people your pup is interacting with. Volunteer roles can also help you when it comes time to find a job.

As you can see, volunteering changes the lives of the people you are helping. It also changes your life. You will expand your horizons while sharing your gifts with the world. It will help you become a more compassionate and caring person. Volunteering with your beloved canine companion will also help you strengthen the bond between the two of you.

 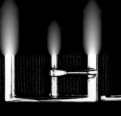

TEXT-DEPENDENT QUESTIONS

1. What are the benefits of volunteering?
2. What are some characteristics that a great therapy dog should have?
3. How can you tell whether your dog is well suited to therapy work?

RESEARCH PROJECT

Using the internet, find a local therapy dog organization and contact it to set up an interview with someone who volunteers as part of a therapy dog team. This interview can be in person or via email. Write a one-page report on what that person does and why they enjoy doing this kind of work.

basic obedience training: teaching an animal basic skills such as sitting, lying down, and staying on command

Canine Good Citizen: a title offered by the AKC that shows a dog has mastered the skills required for it to function politely in human society

foundational skills: fundamental skills that are required to move on to more advanced work

CHAPTER 5

Training a Therapy Dog

Therapy Dog Training and Certification

Once you've determined that both you and your pup are suitable for therapy dog work, you will want to begin the training process. The most important thing you can do is ensure your pet has received proper socialization and **basic obedience training.** This lays the foundation for any further work that you will do with your dog.

According to the Alliance of Therapy Dogs, therapy dogs must be socialized and trusted by people to be successful. As such, puppies should have pleasant and nonthreatening encounters with new people as often as possible. Interactions should happen with well-behaved children, people in uniform, and people wearing hats and glasses. If you're training an adult dog, socialization is still incredibly important. It just may be a little more difficult to get your dog used to strange people and situations (and if this is the case, your dog may not be well suited to this type of work).

No matter the age of your potential therapy dog, you will want to ensure that it has mastered basic obedience commands such as sit, down, leave it, and watch me, and that it is trained to walk on a loose leash and not jump up on people. These **foundational skills** ensure that your pup is well mannered and pleasant to be around. It also ensures that the animal and the people it encounters are kept safe. You can enroll your dog in a basic obedience class, or you can teach it at home.

Pursuing the AKC's **Canine Good Citizen** (CGC) title is an excellent step toward therapy work. In fact, some therapy dog training and certification programs require that you already have it before you begin training or become certified. The CGC program involves dogs learning ten skills. Trainers focus on teaching the basics of good manners and obedience and strengthening the bond between handler and dog. In addition, trainers teach responsible dog ownership.

While you can train your pup for the test at home, there are also classes available that will help you prepare. Dogs are evaluated on several skills:

Scan this code to view a video about how to get your dog ready for therapy dog training.

- Accepting a friendly stranger
- Sitting while being petted
- Walking on a loose leash
- Walking through a crowd
- Following simple commands
- Reacting calmly when separated from its owner
- Coming when called
- Sitting and staying
- Reacting positively to dogs and other distractions
- Remaining still while being groomed

Once your pup passes the test, you will receive paperwork that you can send to the AKC so that its title and certification can be properly registered.

Once your dog has obtained its CGC title, you can move on to the Advanced CGC (CGCA). This title is also known as the AKC Community Canine. Your pup will be tested out in the real world on the skills it learned for its CGC title. If your dog will be working in an urban environment, you can also pursue the AKC Urban CGC title. Working for these titles allows you to develop skills that will be necessary to begin therapy dog training. The titles also allow you to

Many therapy dog certification programs require that a dog has already passed the Canine Good Citizen (CGC) exam, which tests 10 learned skills. One of the skills tested in a CGC exam is your dog's ability to stay in place.

prove to potential work sites that your dog actually has the training required to be a therapy animal.

After your dog has mastered the skills required for the CGC titles, you should enroll your pet in a class for therapy dogs. This type of class is helpful not only for your pup but also for you. It will prepare both of you for what to expect while on visits. The best way to find these classes in your area is to look online. The AKC has a list of both national organizations and local therapy groups on its website. Once you've found one you'd like to work with, you can contact it to learn more about therapy dog classes. A great number of these groups perform a therapy dog evaluation test on you and your dog once you've completed the classes.

Upon passing the evaluation, you will be able to register with one of the national therapy dog organizations. There are some that have partnered with the AKC in developing the Therapy Dog title. Once you've registered with the organization and passed any certifications that it requires, you will be able to apply for the AKC Therapy Dog title. These organizations include the Alliance of Therapy Dogs, Bright and Beautiful Therapy Dogs, Love on a Leash, Pet Partners, and Therapy Dogs International. While the AKC Therapy Dog title isn't a requirement, it can help in establishing that you and your pup are a legitimate therapy animal team.

Once you've gone through the entire process to have your pup certified as a therapy dog, the organization you decided to work with will be able to connect you with facilities and other places where you can volunteer. Alternatively, you can reach out to potential volunteer sites on your own and ask if they would be open to allowing a therapy dog team to work at their location. No matter where you decide to volunteer, you and your pet will be able to touch people's lives.

Emotional Support Animal Training and Certification

As discussed in a previous chapter, emotional support animals are not required to have any sort of training or certification.

While emtional support animals are not required to have certifications, they should be well-trained. For example, an emotional support dog should be able to walk on a loose leash.

However, this doesn't mean that you should not have a well-trained emotional support dog. You want your pet to be able to respond to your emotional needs when necessary. A dog that is unable to follow basic obedience commands such as sit, stay, down, and heel will not have the foundation required to assist you on command.

In addition, basic obedience training makes your dog more pleasant to be around, both at home and in public. A dog that barks and lunges at strange people or animals isn't an ideal choice. If your pup already exhibits these kinds of behaviors, you will need to work with a professional to train them out of your pet.

Once your dog has mastered the basics, you may wish to teach it how to apply deep pressure therapy (DPT). This type of therapy is a proven way to relieve emotional and mental distress. According to the website NurseBuff, DPT involves application of gentle pressure to the chest area. Owners can train the dog to climb onto the chest to apply pressure to calm them.

Training your pup will ensure that it is well behaved and able to perform its job no matter where you may be. Since many people fly with their emotional support dogs, you want to be sure that your pup will behave appropriately on the flight. You also want your animal to calmly perform its comforting job when you are in locations outside of your home.

In addition to training your pup, you will want to ensure that it is well socialized. Your emotional support animal should be welcoming and friendly toward people it doesn't know, as well as toward other animals. If you choose an emotional support dog that has a calm and friendly temperament, you won't have to do a whole lot of training in this regard.

While certification isn't a requirement, it is highly recommended that you obtain it. This will help you find housing in rentals that have no-pet policies. It will also make it easier for you to take your pet on an airline flight without being charged a pet fee. Before you can certify your emotional support animal, you will need to have a diagnosis from a licensed mental health care provider. This person can then prescribe an emotional support animal. This is usually done via a letter.

After this, you can apply for an emotional support certification with a registration organization. You will typically receive a letter and an identification card. These will be used to show landlords and airlines that your animal is a legitimate emotional support dog.

Remember, having an emotional support dog does not entitle you to take your dog into businesses and other spaces. The only privileges are the right to rent anywhere and the right to have your pup fly on an airline with you at no cost. This means that you should check before bringing your animal other places.

Emotional support dogs can be trained to provide deep pressure therapy to their owners.

Therapy dogs are not just used in the home. They also offer much-needed comfort in schools, hospitals and nursing homes and even in workplaces. Therapy dogs are important in schools because they help students focus and connect more in class, as well as relieve anxiety that a student may feel in the classroom. Therapy dogs can motivate students to learn, and research has shown that therapy dogs even increase school attendance.

Hospital stays can cause anxiety, and therapy dogs offer optimism and joy to patients. Therapy dogs are a welcome site in both waiting rooms and hospital rooms, and as a result, many hospitals have adopted the practice.

Therapy dogs are very beneficial in nursing homes. The elderly patients often feel lonely and anxious and a therapy dog can be very helpful and healing. These pups improve morale and decrease feelings of loneliness. Some nursing homes allow patients to have their own pets with them, but many of the residents do not want to or cannot take on the responsibility of full-time care of an animal. Therapy dogs are a great way to have the benefits of companionship without the added responsibility.

Wouldn't it be fun to have a dog in the workplace? Many companies already allow employees to bring dogs to work on some days, but more and more workplaces are also using licensed therapy dogs. These dogs help employees lower stress levels and react better to stressful situations. These pups boost employee morale and make the workplace a more enjoyable place to be.

Regardless of where therapy dogs work, they offer tremendous mental and physical health benefits. Just petting an animal creates an automatic relaxation response in humans. Studies have shown that interaction with animals promotes the release of certain mood-elevating hormones. These dogs increase mental stimulation and are often used to help memory recall in patients with diseases like dementia and Alzheimer's disease.

Therapy dogs help lower blood pressure and slow breathing in anxious people. Children with autism often feel a deep bond with animals, and a therapy dog can help these children better interact with humans, something they sometimes find difficulty with.

While an emotional support animal works with one person, it should also be well socialized so that interactions with strangers go smoothly.

The Joy That Therapy and Emotional Support Animals Bring

As you've learned, therapy and emotional support dogs bring a great deal of comfort and happiness to people in need of support. They willingly give of themselves to help people going through traumatic or stressful events to cope. These amazing animals help children, teenagers, and college students relieve their stress throughout the school year. They bring joy to people who are confined in hospitals or nursing homes. No matter what setting they find themselves in, they prove over and over again that dogs are truly man's best friend, always willing to lend a comforting paw to help us get through life.

Once you've completed the training process, you and your pup will be able to touch people's lives in a positive way.

TALLY: COLLEGE COUNSELOR

Students enrolled at Lesley University in Cambridge, Massachusetts, get an extra perk when they visit the university's Counseling Center. This perk comes in the form of Tally, who was adopted by Counseling Center Director Magi McKinnies in 2014. McKinnies spent time ensuring that Tally was exposed to people of different abilities and ages. This prepared her to spend her days at the Counseling Center waiting for students to come by for pets and cuddles.

While Tally is there to assist students, faculty, and staff members who are utilizing the Counseling Center's services, she is available for everyone to drop by and see her for a quick cuddle session. McKinnies says that many students drop by before exams to have a session with the animal because they find it calms their nerves and helps to relieve their stress. The dog typically takes part in McKinnies's counseling sessions and has proven to be a great comfort to students. One student even claimed that Tally was the reason they decided to go to Lesley University.

Ellen O'Neill, the Counseling Center's administrative assistant, has witnessed the soothing effect that Tally has on those who come to visit with her. She recalls a time when a student dropped by to sit with Tally. O'Neill says that the student had clearly been upset but came out of the session with Tally very relaxed.

Therapy and emotional support animals bring joy wherever they go.

TEXT-DEPENDENT QUESTIONS

1. What skills are tested for the CGC title?
2. What two things should you do to prepare your pet for therapy dog training?
3. What is deep pressure therapy?

RESEARCH PROJECT

Choose a therapy dog organization and research its requirements for a dog to become certified. Develop a PowerPoint presentation for your class on the process.

Americans with Disabilities Act (ADA): legislation in the United States that prohibits discrimination against people with disabilities (Therapy Dogs)

basic obedience training: teaching an animal basic skills such as sitting, laying down, and staying on command (Therapy Dogs)

Canine Good Citizen: a title offered by the AKC that shows a dog has mastered the skills required for it to function politely in human society (Therapy Dogs)

cardiovascular: relating to the heart and blood vessels (Therapy Dogs)

caveat: a warning of certain limitations (Therapy Dogs)

cognitive: relating to or involving conscious intellectual activity (Therapy Dogs)

executive functioning: the cognitive ability to plan, focus, remember, and juggle several tasks at a time (Therapy Dogs)

Fair Housing Act: legislation in the United States that prohibits discrimination against someone renting or buying a house (Therapy Dogs)

foundational skills: fundamental skills that are required to move on to more advanced work (Therapy Dogs)

legitimate: legally allowed or acceptable (Therapy Dogs)

neurological: relating to the nerves and nervous system (Therapy Dogs)

objectively: not influenced by your personal feelings or opinions (Therapy Dogs)

psychological: relating to or affecting the mental or emotional state of a person (Therapy Dogs)

self-esteem: confidence in yourself, or the feeling that you are valuable; self-worth (Therapy Dogs)

sociable: willing to engage with others (Therapy Dogs)

social-emotional skills: the ability to understand, experience, manage, and express emotions (Therapy Dogs)

ORGANIZATIONS TO CONTACT

American Kennel Club Headquarters
101 Park Avenue, New York, NY 10178
Phone: (212) 696-8200
Website: https://www.akc.org/

The Association of Professional Dog Trainers (APDT)
2365 Harrodsburg Road A325
Lexington, KY 40504
Phone: 1-800-PET-DOGS
Email: membership@adpt.com
Website: https://apdt.com

Pet Partners
345 118th Ave. SE
Suite 200
Bellevue, WA 98005
Phone: (425) 679-5500
Website: https://www.petpartners.org

Therapy Dogs International
88 Bartley Road
Flanders, NJ 07836
Phone: (973) 252-9800
Fax: (973) 252-7171
Email: tdi@gti.net
Website: https://www.tdi-dog.org

US Department of Justice
950 Pennsylvania Avenue, NW
Civil Rights Division
Disability Rights Section – NYA
Washington, DC 20530
Phone: (202) 307-0663
Fax: (202) 307-1197
Website: https://www.ada.gov/

BOOKS

Bauer, Jean. *Joy Unleashed: The Story of Bella, the Unlikely Therapy Dog.* New York, NY: Skyhorse Publishing, 2016.

Binfet, John-Tyler, and Elizabeth Kjellstrand Hartwig. *Canine-Assisted Interventions: A Comprehensive Guide to Credentialing Therapy Dog Teams.* New York, NY: Routledge, 2020.

Hiland, Victoria. *Emotional Support Animals: The Ins and Outs of ESAs.* Independently Published, 2017.

Howie, Ann R. *Teaming with Your Therapy Dog.* West Lafayette, IN: Purdue University Press, 2015.

Lutes, Linda. *Pogo's Tale: The Life of a Therapy Dog.* Prescott, AZ: Leapin' Lizards Press, 2018.

WEBSITES

AKC Canine Good Citizen Program
American Kennel Club
Website: https://www.akc.org/products-services/training-programs/canine-good-citizen/

AKC Therapy Dog Program
Email: akctherapydog@akc.org
Website: https://www.akc.org/products-services/training-programs/akc-therapy-dog-program/

Alliance of Therapy Dogs
Website: https://www.therapydogs.com

INDEX

HEATHER PIDCOCK-REED holds a master's degree in professional writing from Chatham University, where she studied topics such as science and environmental writing, political and news writing, technical writing, teaching technical writing, and writing for digital media. She also holds a BFA from the Academy of Art University in motion pictures and television with an emphasis in screenwriting. Heather's main interests lie in education, journalism, writing for digital media, and, of course, dogs. Her previous publications include *Contemporary Issues: Immigration* and *Contemporary Issues: Environment.* She currently resides in La Junta, Colorado, with her five dogs.

CREDITS